MW01206522

This notebook belongs to:

____

Made in the USA
Las Vegas, NV
01 December 2023

81944552R00066